I0759891
TOP 10
LOUDEST
ANIMALS
Children's Press®
An imprint of Scholastic Inc.
BY BRENNA MALONEY

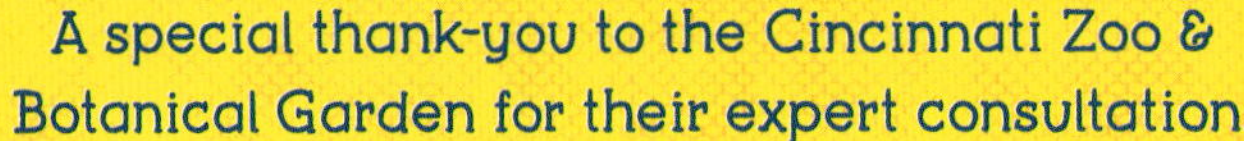

A special thank-you to the Cincinnati Zoo & Botanical Garden for their expert consultation.

Copyright © 2026 by Scholastic Inc.

All rights reserved. Published by Children's Press, an imprint of Scholastic Inc., *Publishers since 1920.* SCHOLASTIC, CHILDREN'S PRESS, and associated logos are trademarks and/or registered trademarks of Scholastic Inc.

The publisher does not have any control over and does not assume any responsibility for author or third-party websites or their content.

No part of this publication may be reproduced, stored in a retrieval system, or transmitted in any form or by any means, electronic, mechanical, photocopying, recording, or otherwise, or used to train any artificial intelligence technologies, without written permission of the publisher. For information regarding permission, write to Scholastic Inc., Attention: Permissions Department, 557 Broadway, New York, NY 10012.

Library of Congress Cataloging-in-Publication Data available

ISBN 978-1-5461-7780-7 (library binding)
ISBN 978-1-5461-7781-4 (paperback)

10 9 8 7 6 5 4 3 2 1 26 27 28 29 30

Printed in China 62
First edition, 2026

Book design by Kay Petronio

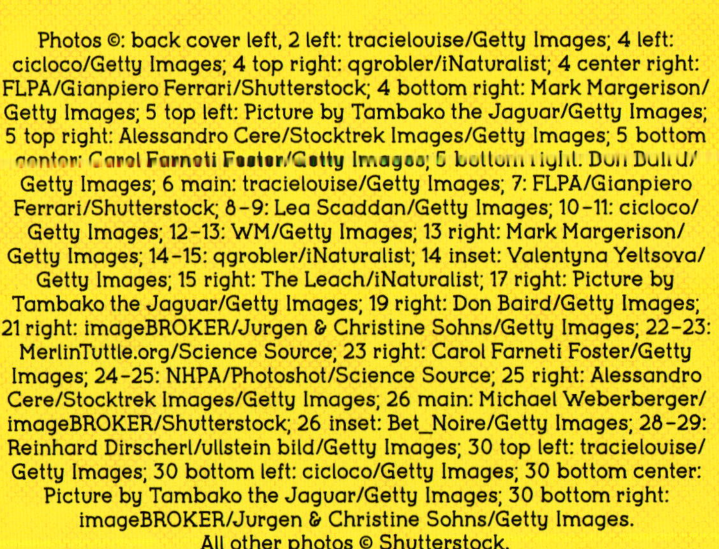

Photos ©: back cover left, 2 left: tracielouise/Getty Images; 4 left: cicloco/Getty Images; 4 top right: qgrobler/iNaturalist; 4 center right: FLPA/Gianpiero Ferrari/Shutterstock; 4 bottom right: Mark Margerison/Getty Images; 5 top left: Picture by Tambako the Jaguar/Getty Images; 5 top right: Alessandro Cere/Stocktrek Images/Getty Images; 5 bottom center: Carol Farneti Foster/Getty Images; 5 bottom right: Don Baird/Getty Images; 6 main: tracielouise/Getty Images; 7: FLPA/Gianpiero Ferrari/Shutterstock; 8–9: Lea Scaddan/Getty Images; 10–11: cicloco/Getty Images; 12–13: WM/Getty Images; 13 right: Mark Margerison/Getty Images; 14–15: qgrobler/iNaturalist; 14 inset: Valentyna Yeltsova/Getty Images; 15 right: The Leach/iNaturalist; 17 right: Picture by Tambako the Jaguar/Getty Images; 19 right: Don Baird/Getty Images; 21 right: imageBROKER/Jurgen & Christine Sohns/Getty Images; 22–23: MerlinTuttle.org/Science Source; 23 right: Carol Farneti Foster/Getty Images; 24–25: NHPA/Photoshot/Science Source; 25 right: Alessandro Cere/Stocktrek Images/Getty Images; 26 main: Michael Weberberger/imageBROKER/Shutterstock; 26 inset: Bet_Noire/Getty Images; 28–29: Reinhard Dirscherl/ullstein bild/Getty Images; 30 top left: tracielouise/Getty Images; 30 bottom left: cicloco/Getty Images; 30 bottom center: Picture by Tambako the Jaguar/Getty Images; 30 bottom right: imageBROKER/Jurgen & Christine Sohns/Getty Images. All other photos © Shutterstock.

SPERM WHALE

CONTENTS

LOUD AND PROUD

Some animals make a lot of noise! They bark, growl, chirp, or squawk. Some also sing, click, cackle, or howl. They make sounds to talk to each other. They make sounds to scare away **predators**.

Some animals even make sounds to find a **mate** or protect their home. But not all animals make the same amount of noise. Are you ready to learn which animal is the loudest? Read on and count down from ten to one. Let's find out which animal takes the top spot!

#10 LAUGHING KOOKABURRA (KUK-uh-bur-uh)

FACT FILE

ANIMAL GROUP: Bird

HABITAT: Forests

AVERAGE SIZE: A bowling pin

DIET: **Carnivore**

AS LOUD AS: A motorcycle

The laughing kookaburra is known for its loud call. But there is nothing funny about the sound it makes. The kookaburra's cackle is a warning to other birds.

The sound means "Stay away!" One kookaburra will make the sound. Then birds from its family will join in. This lets other birds know that this spot is taken! Kookaburras use softer sounds to find a mate.

FACT

A kookaburra's laugh can be heard for miles.

LAUGHING KOOKABURRA CLOSE-UP

BODY

A thick body supports its large head.

FEATHERS

Brown-and-white feathers blend in with its environment.

TAIL

When this bird calls, its tail feathers fan out.

HEAD
Its feathers come to a small crest on its head.
EYES
These birds can spot prey from far away.
BILL
A sharp bill is black on top. It is light brown on the bottom.
FACT
A kookaburra's call can be mistaken for a monkey's!

#9 HOWLER MONKEY

FACT FILE

ANIMAL GROUP: Mammal

HABITAT: Rainforests

AVERAGE SIZE: A large backpack

DIET: Herbivore

AS LOUD AS: A lawnmower

Howler monkeys are the loudest of all monkeys. They call out to claim their area. And to keep predators away. Their loud calls sound like big, whooping barks.

One group of howler monkeys will call out. Then another group will answer. Howler monkeys like to start and end their days by calling to each other. They will also howl during rainstorms.

FACT

A large bone in their throat makes howler monkeys so loud.

FACT FILE

ANIMAL GROUP: **Amphibian**

HABITAT: Forests

AVERAGE SIZE: A Ping-Pong ball

DIET: Carnivore

AS LOUD AS: A subway train

The coqui is the loudest frog in the world! Males use their sound to attract mates. Males will challenge each other to a song battle.

The frog that loses the singing contest must leave the area. The frog that wins can stay with its new mate. Coqui frogs sing at any time of day. But they are most vocal at night.

FACT "Coqui" is also the sound these frogs make. *Koh-KEE! Koh-KEE!*

A coqui's throat swells when it makes a sound.

#7 CICADA

FACT FILE

ANIMAL GROUP: **Invertebrate**

HABITATS: Forests, grasslands, savannas

AVERAGE SIZE: A key chain

DIET: Herbivore

AS LOUD AS: A jackhammer

Cicadas make the loudest sound in the insect world! Male cicadas use song to attract a mate. To be loud, male cicadas move special parts of their bodies.

They have a thin layer covering their bellies. Little **muscles** help pull this layer in and out quickly. The vibration makes their buzzing song. The sound is even louder because the cicada's belly is mostly hollow.

FACT

Female cicadas make clicking sounds by flicking their wings.

#6 SPOTTED HYENA

FACT FILE

ANIMAL GROUP: Mammal

HABITATS: Grasslands, savannas

AVERAGE SIZE: A large dog

DIET: Omnivore

AS LOUD AS: A chainsaw

Spotted hyenas make lots of different sounds. They bark, cluck, groan, grunt, and yowl. They even make a noise that sounds like laughter.

But when a hyena "laughs," it's not because it's happy. Hyenas laugh when they feel scared or upset. They also make a whooping sound that is special to each hyena. They make this sound to let other hyenas know they are there!

FACT Hyenas also laugh after they catch prey.

#5 LION

FACT FILE

ANIMAL GROUP: Mammal

HABITATS: Grasslands, savannas

AVERAGE SIZE: A large sofa

DIET: Carnivore

AS LOUD AS: A car horn

When a lion roars, everyone listens! Lions have the loudest roar of all the big cats. This sound is a deep rumble. It can make the ground shake.

Lions need space to hunt, raise their cubs, and find food and water. A lion's roar warns other animals. It means "This space belongs to us." Lions also roar to talk to each other in their pride. A pride is their family group.

FACT

A lion's roar can be heard from 5 miles (8 km) away. That is more than 70 football fields!

#4 NORTHERN ELEPHANT SEAL

FACT FILE

ANIMAL GROUP: Mammal

HABITAT: Coastal waters

AVERAGE SIZE: A small car

DIET: Carnivore

AS LOUD AS: A thunderclap

Male northern elephant seals are really loud! Their big, trunk-like noses make their voices sound even louder. This is similar to what an elephant's trunk does.

When they sense danger, these seals make a low chuffing sound. Then they let out a deep, thundering roar. Male seals are also very strong. They will fight each other to find a mate. Each seal has its own voice that other seals can recognize.

FACT

Females make softer calls to their pups. The pups answer with squeaky cries.

#3 GREATER BULLDOG BAT

FACT FILE

ANIMAL GROUP: Mammal

HABITATS: Ponds and streams

AVERAGE SIZE: A football

DIET: Carnivore

AS LOUD AS: A jet engine

The greater bulldog bat makes clicking sounds while hunting. It is looking for bugs flying in the air. And for fish swimming in the water.

The bat's loud clicks bounce off flying insects. They bounce off ripples in the water made by fish. The sounds come back to the bat. This tells the bat exactly where its prey is. Then it can catch something to eat!

FACT

The way these bats hunt with sound is called **echolocation**.

#2 SNAPPING SHRIMP

FACT FILE

ANIMAL GROUP: Invertebrate

HABITAT: Waters, like those with coral reefs

AVERAGE SIZE: A clothespin

DIET: Carnivore

AS LOUD AS: A volcanic eruption

Snapping shrimp make a LOUD sound with their larger claw. These shrimp wait for fish to swim by. When they sense one, they open this big claw.

The claw fills up with water. When the claw closes, water shoots out very quickly. This creates a powerful bubble. When this bubble bursts, it kills what's in its path. And it creates a super-loud sound.

FACT

This animal is also called a pistol shrimp. Its claw snaps shut as fast as a bullet leaving a pistol.

Claw

#1 SPERM WHALE

FACT FILE

ANIMAL GROUP: Mammal

HABITAT: Oceans

AVERAGE SIZE: A school bus

DIET: Carnivore

AS LOUD AS: A rocket launch

Which animal is the loudest? It is the sperm whale! It makes clicking sounds and creaks. These sounds travel through two flaps inside the whale's head.

These flaps clap together to make the loud sound. The whale uses these sounds to talk to other whales. It also uses sounds to find food. The sounds bounce off things like squid or fish. These sounds return to the whale. Now it can locate its prey.

FACT A sperm whale can find a squid more than 1 mile (1.6 km) away with sound. They use echolocation.

BRAIN

The sperm whale has the largest brain on Earth. It is more than five times heavier than a human's!

BLOWHOLE

The blowhole is shaped like an S. It is on the front of the head.

EYES

Its eyes help the whale see light and shadows.

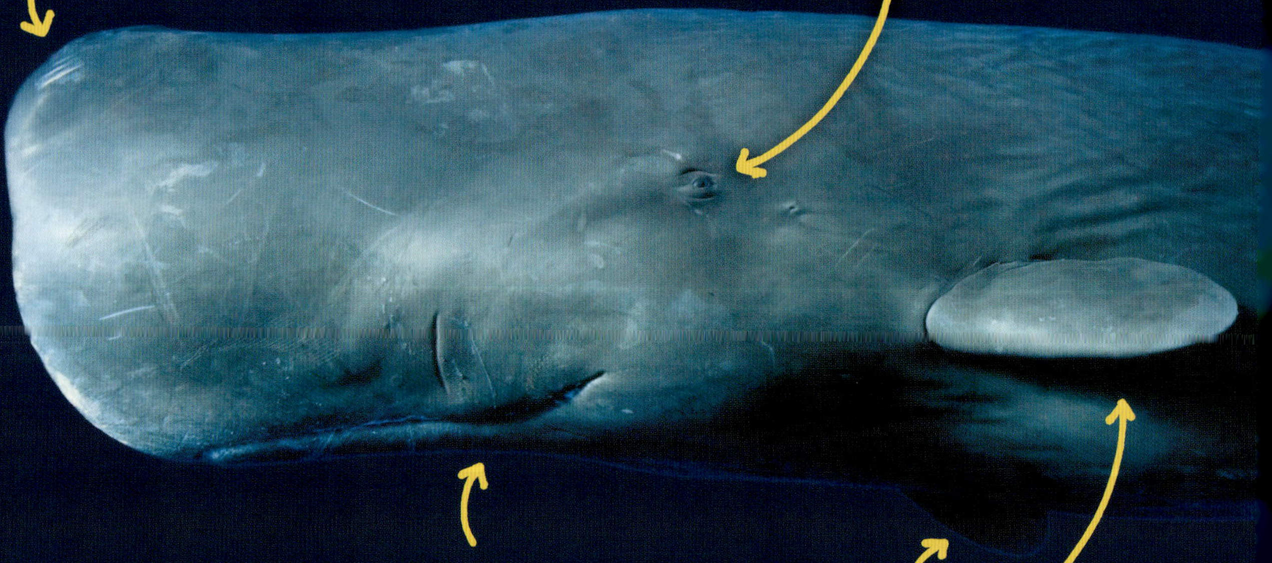

JAW

The long, lower jaw is filled with teeth.

FLIPPERS

Both flippers are small and round.

SPERM WHALE CLOSE-UP

BACK

A low fin in the whale's back looks like a hump. Bumpy nobs line its lower back.

TAIL

The end of the tail is divided into two triangles. They help the whale swim.

SKIN

Its dark gray skin is wrinkly, like a raisin.

FACT The pattern of clicks a sperm whale makes is called a coda.

SIZING THEM UP

There are many loud animals on Earth! Being loud helps them. That is how they talk to each other. That is also how they defend themselves and protect their homes. When you're outside, keep your ears open. Listen to loud noises that other animals make. Then you can create your own list!

GLOSSARY

amphibian (am-FIB-ee-uhn) a cold-blooded animal with a backbone that lives in water and breathes with gills when young

carnivore (KAHR-nuh-vor) an animal that eats meat

crest (krest) a tuft of feathers on the top of a bird's head

crustacean (kruh-STAY-shuhn) a sea creature that has an outer skeleton, such as a crab, lobster, or shrimp

echolocation (ek-oh-loh-KAY-shuhn) the process for locating objects by reflected sound waves

herbivore (HUR-buh-vor) an animal that only eats plants

invertebrate (in-VUR-tuh-brit) an animal without a backbone

mammal (MAM-uhl) a warm-blooded animal that has fur and usually gives birth to live babies

mate the male or female partner of a pair of animals

muscle (MUHS-uhl) a type of tissue in a body that can contract to produce movement

omnivore (AHM-nuh-vor) an animal that eats both plants and meat

predator (PRED-uh-tur) an animal that lives by hunting other animals for food

prey (pray) an animal that is hunted by another animal for food

INDEX

Page numbers in **bold** indicate images.

ABOUT THE AUTHOR

Brenna Maloney is the author of many books. She lives in Washington, DC, with her husband and two sons. She laughs a lot, so sometimes she sounds like a hyena.